GRUESOME GOBLINS

I0810834

FANTASY CREATURES

Gareth Stevens PUBLISHING

HOT TOPICS

BY BENJAMIN PROUDFIT

Please visit our website, www.garethstevens.com. For a free color catalog of all our high-quality books, call toll free 1-800-542-2595 or fax 1-877-542-2596.

Library of Congress Cataloging-in-Publication Data
Names: Proudfit, Benjamin author
Title: Gruesome goblins / Benjamin Proudfit.
Description: Buffalo, NY : Gareth Stevens Publishing, [2026] | Series: Fantasy creatures | Includes index.
Identifiers: LCCN 2025020098 (print) | LCCN 2025020099 (ebook) | ISBN 9781482475258 (library binding) | ISBN 9781482475241 (paperback) | ISBN 9781482475265 (ebook)
Subjects: LCSH: Goblins | Goblins–Folklore–Juvenile literature | Goblins in art
Classification: LCC GR549 .P76 2026 (print) | LCC GR549 (ebook) | DDC 398.21–dc23/eng/20250621
LC record available at https://lccn.loc.gov/2025020098
LC ebook record available at https://lccn.loc.gov/2025020099

Published in 2026 by
Gareth Stevens Publishing
2544 Clinton Street
Buffalo, NY 14224

Copyright © 2026 Gareth Stevens Publishing

Designer: Leslie Taylor
Editor: Kristen Nelson

Photo credits: Cover (goblin), 5, 7 Shutterstock AI Generator/Shutterstock.com; cover and series art (neon circle) Ikrill/Shutterstock.com, (rough frame) TarnishArt/Shutterstock.com, (splotchy background) TiffanyShanks/Shutterstock.com; p. 9 (goblin) John Dickson Batten/File:Goblin illustration from 19th century.png_commons.wikimedia.org, (fairy) Passion-pearl/Shutterstock.com, (leprechaun) createvil/Shutterstock.com; p. 11 (castle) stocksolutions/Shutterstock.com, (redcap goblin) Vector Contributor Danilo Sanino/Shutterstock.com, (inset bottom right) Willy Pogány/File:The Little white feather.jpeg_commons.wikimedia.org; p. 13 Keith Tarrier/Shutterstock.com; p. 15 Doodeez/Shutterstock.com; p. 16 Morphart Creation/Shutterstock.com; p. 17 User:Edelseider/File:Hans Christian Andersen Stærekassen - cropped.jpg_commons.wikimedia.org; p. 18 Erman Gunes/Shutterstock.com; p. 19 Heather Paul/Flickr.com; p. 21 Aisyaqilumaranas/Shutterstock.com; p. 23 (game) Niferure/Shutterstock.com, (inset) Shutterstock AI Generator/Shutterstock.com; p. 25 vvoe/Shutterstock.com; p. 27 RichartPhotos/Shutterstock.com; p. 29 Arthur Rackham/File:Goblin Market 002.jpg_commons.wikimedia.org; p. 30 (Goblin Combe) Adam Cli/File:Goblin Combe AWT 2.jpg_commons.wikimedia.org, (Goblin Valley) donarreiskoffer/File:Goblin Valley State Park (4).JPG_commons.wikimedia.org, (Yester Castle) Helspence/File:Yester Castle 01.jpg_commons.wikimedia.org, (Goblin Bay) Film Adventure/Shutterstock.com, (Goblin planet) Natalllenka.m/Shutterstock.com.

Some of the images in this book illustrate individuals who are models. The depictions do not imply actual situations or events.

All rights reserved. No part of this book may be reproduced in any form without permission in writing from the publisher, except by a reviewer.

Printed in China

CPSIA compliance information: Batch #QWGS26: For further information contact Gareth Stevens, at 1-800-542-2595.

Find us on

CONTENTS

What Makes a Goblin? 4

Goblins in Europe 8

Asian Goblins 12

Fairy Tales 14

Tolkien's Take 18

Pop Culture Goblins 20

Get Creative! 28

Places Named "Goblin" 30

For More Information 31

Glossary 32

Index 32

What Makes a Goblin?

What looks a bit like a small human, but is sneaky, ugly, and maybe a bit evil too? These are all features of goblins! These **fantasy** creatures have been part of stories for hundreds of years.

IMAGINE THAT!

SOME STORIES SAY GOBLINS ARE A MEAN KIND OF FAIRY.

Goblin stories, or those about goblin-like creatures, have been told all over the world. These stories have long been used to scare children into good **behavior**. Goblins may have some magical or **supernatural** abilities that help them make mischief, or trouble!

IMAGINE THAT!

GOBLINS ARE COMMONLY SAID TO LIVE IN DARK PLACES, SUCH AS UNDERGROUND.

Goblins in Europe

Trouble-making goblins are found in the tales of many places in Europe. Goblins are sometimes said to have come from France. In fact, French writers were some of the first to include goblins in literature, or written works.

IMAGINE THAT!

OTHER FANTASY CREATURES OF EUROPEAN TALES INCLUDE LEPRECHAUNS, GNOMES, AND FAIRIES. UNLIKE GOBLINS, THESE CREATURES MAKE FUN MISCHIEF—NOT EVIL TROUBLE!

There are many stories of goblin-like creatures in the history of the United Kingdom. One story says the redcap lives in broken down castles in England and Scotland. They attack travelers! Redcaps use blood to make their caps red.

IMAGINE THAT!

THE GERMAN WORD FOR GOBLIN IS KOBOLD. THESE CREATURES LIVE UNDERGROUND AND PLAY MEAN TRICKS. SOMETIMES THEY KEEP BOTHERING ONE FAMILY!

HERMITAGE CASTLE
IN SCOTLAND
REDCAP
KOBOLD

Asian Goblins

In Japan, goblin-like creatures known as *tengu* are said to live in the mountains. They may be able to **shapeshift**. They often cause trouble, such as taking children. *Tengu* are shown with long noses and red faces.

IMAGINE THAT!

IN KOREAN TALES, GOBLINS CALLED *DOKKAEBI* PLAY TRICKS AND CAN DO A LITTLE MAGIC.

TENGU

Fairy Tales

In the early 1800s, Jacob and Wilhelm Grimm put out books of fairy tales. Some had goblins in them! "The Goblins" tells of a woman whose child is taken by goblins. They put a changeling in its place. She had to make the changeling laugh to get her baby back!

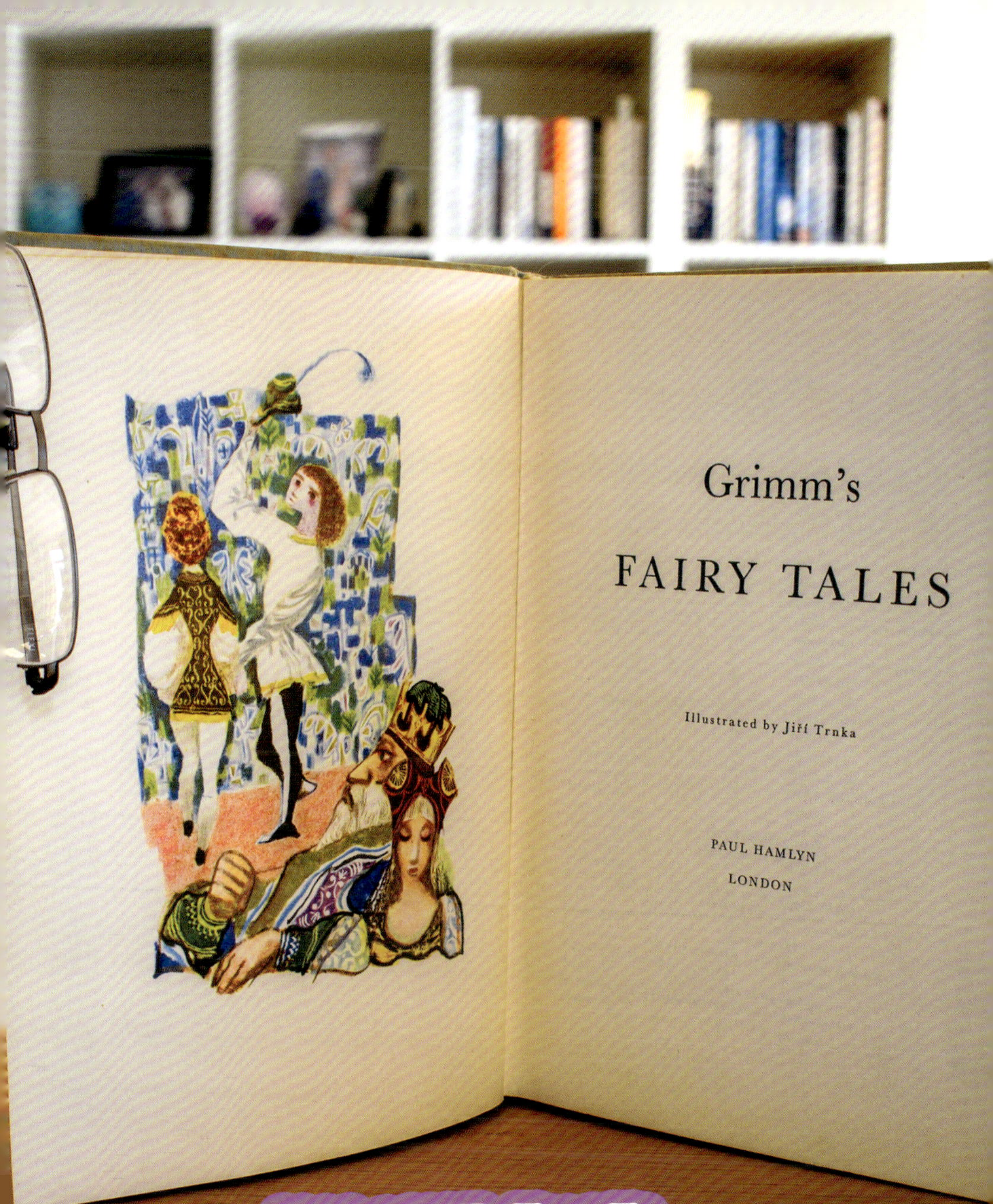

IMAGINE THAT!

A CHANGELING IS THE WEAK CHILD OF A SUPERNATURAL BEING, LIKE A FAIRY, THAT IS PUT IN THE PLACE OF A HUMAN CHILD THAT HAS BEEN STOLEN.

Fairy-tale writer Hans Christian Andersen wrote about goblins too. In the 1850s, he wrote "The Goblin and the Huckster," sometimes called "The Goblin and the Grocer." A goblin cuts out a woman's tongue in this story!

IMAGINE THAT!

ANDERSEN ALSO WROTE "THE PRINCESS AND THE PEA," "THE SNOW QUEEN," AND "THE LITTLE MERMAID."

HANS CHRISTIAN ANDERSEN

Tolkien's Take

J. R. R. Tolkien wrote about goblins in his 1937 book *The Hobbit*. He named the leader of the goblins the Great Goblin. He sat upon a throne of stone in the Misty Mountains and had a big head!

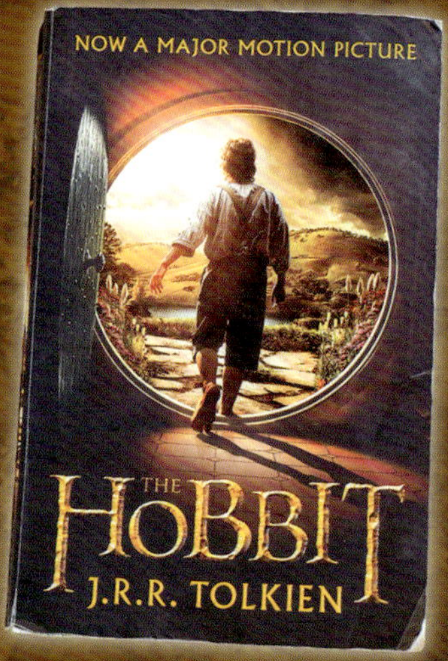

IMAGINE THAT!

IN TOLKIEN'S *LORD OF THE RINGS* BOOKS, HE USES A DIFFERENT WORD FOR GOBLINS: ORCS. THEY WERE MEAN, UGLY, AND HATED BY JUST ABOUT EVERYONE.

ORC

Pop Culture Goblins

The Spider-Man villain, or bad guy, Green Goblin first appeared in the *Amazing Spider-Man* comics in 1964. He was born when a man named Norman Osborn took a mix of **chemicals** called the Goblin Formula. It makes Osborn stronger and faster—but he loses his mind!

GREEN GOBLIN

IMAGINE THAT!

OTHER SPIDER-MAN VILLAINS TAKE AFTER GREEN GOBLIN, INCLUDING RED GOBLIN, GOBLIN KING, AND HOBGOBLIN.

Fantasy games often feature goblins. The goblins in the tabletop game **Dungeons & Dragons** are small, evil, humanlike beings. They hide in dungeons and similar places. On their own, they can't do much. But groups of goblins can cause trouble in the game.

IMAGINE THAT!

THE TABLETOP GAME WARHAMMER INCLUDES A FEW KINDS OF GOBLINS: COMMON GOBLINS, NIGHT GOBLINS, AND FOREST GOBLINS AMONG THEM.

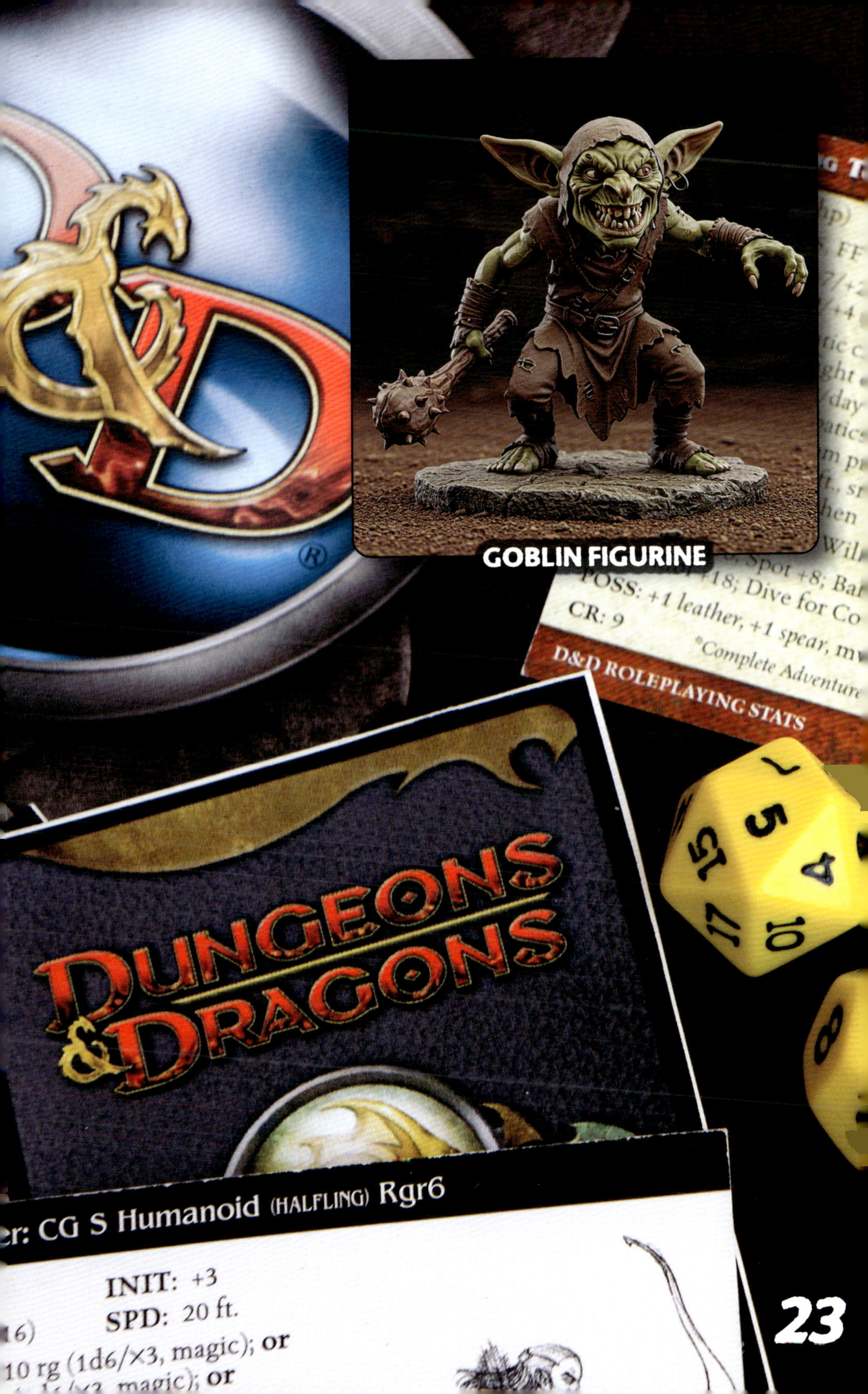

GOBLIN FIGURINE

The trading card game Magic: The Gathering first came out in 1993. Over the history of the game, there have been about 400 different goblin cards! These creatures are often known for causing **chaos** and destroying what they can.

IMAGINE THAT!

SOME FANTASY CREATURES FOUND IN MAGIC AREN'T FROM OTHER FANTASY STORIES. FOR EXAMPLE, THE BEAST CALLED THE MASTICORE IS JUST IN MAGIC.

Mogg Jailer
Creature — Goblin
Mogg Jailer can't attack if defending player controls an untapped creature with power 2 or less.
Hey, wake up!
—Mogg secret password
Illus. Mark Romanoski
©1993–2001 Wizards of the Coast, Inc. 68/143
2/2
ature — Dwarf
rifice Pardic Miner: Target player
't play lands this turn.
Illus. Tony Szczudlo
1/1
ture — Horror
hen Phyrexian Rager
lay, you draw a card a
Illus. Mark Tedin
Two target creatures
until end of tu
get +2/+2
Although the elves of Argoth always considered them a nuisance, the pixies made fine allies during the war against the machines.
Illus. Jeff Mir
©1993–1998 Wizards
Rebirth
Horned Kavu
MAGIC CARDS

Goblins run the wizarding bank, Gringotts, in the *Harry Potter* books and movies. They have some magical abilities and also work with metal. In these stories, goblins mostly live underground. They aren't trusted by the wider magical community.

IMAGINE THAT!

GOBLINS MADE THE SWORD FOR THE FAMOUS *HARRY POTTER* WIZARD, GODRIC GRYFFINDOR.

GRINGOTTS
GOBLIN

Get Creative!

Stories of goblins and beings like goblins have such a long, rich history. Fantasy writers and artists have so many ideas to choose from for their work. But there's always something new to add to old tales! What can you imagine?

IMAGINE THAT!

STORIES OF GOBLINS WOULDN'T BE AS GOOD WITHOUT THE ILLUSTRATIONS, OR PICTURES, THAT GO WITH THEM. THAT'S WHERE ARTISTS COME IN!

ILLUSTRATION FOR THE POEM "GOBLIN MARKET" BY CHRISTINA ROSSETTI

Places Named "Goblin"

GOBLIN COMBE NATURE RESERVE

United Kingdom

This is a beautiful grassland where visitors can hike and view nature.

GOBLIN VALLEY STATE PARK

Utah

Interesting landforms called "goblins" give this park its name.

YESTER CASTLE

Scotland

Part of this castle goes underground to a place known as "Goblin Hall."

GOBLIN BAY

Canada

This small body of water is found near Georgian Bay in Ontario.

THE GOBLIN

deep space

This dwarf, or small, planet is found beyond Neptune in our solar system.

FOR MORE INFORMATION

BOOKS

Munsey, Lizzie, et al. *Supernatural Creatures: Mythical and Sacred Creatures from Around the World.* New York, NY: DK, 2024.

Nardo, Don. *Creatures and Beasts in World Mythology.* San Diego, CA: ReferencePoint Press, Inc., 2025.

WEBSITES

Fantasy Books for Kids
https://www.commonsensemedia.org/lists/fantasy-books-for-kids
Find lots of great fantasy books for kids here.

Fantasy Movies for Kids
https://www.commonsensemedia.org/lists/best-fantasy-movies
Find your next favorite fantasy movie here!

Publisher's note to educators and parents: Our editors have carefully reviewed these websites to ensure that they are suitable for students. Many websites change frequently, however, and we cannot guarantee that a site's future contents will continue to meet our high standards of quality and educational value. Be advised that students should be closely supervised whenever they access the internet.

GLOSSARY

behavior: The way one acts.

chaos: The state of confusion.

chemical: Having to do with matter that when mixed causes changes.

dungeon: A dark prison, usually underground.

fantasy: Having to do with imaginative stories that feature impossible events and characters.

shapeshift: Change form.

supernatural: Unable to be explained or seeming to come from magic.

INDEX

Andersen, Hans Christian, 16

changeling, 14, 15

dokkaebi, 12

Dungeons & Dragons, 22, 23

fairy, 4, 9, 15

features, 4, 6

France, 8

gnome, 9

Green Goblin, 20, 21

Grimm, Jacob, 14

Grimm, Wilhelm, 14

Harry Potter, 26

Hobbit, The, 18

Japan, 12

kobold, 10

leprechaun, 9

Lord of the Rings, 18

Magic, The Gathering, 24

orcs, 18

redcaps, 10

tengu, 12

Tolkien, J. R. R., 18

United Kingdom, 10, 30

Warhammer, 22